DOMINATE YOUR DISTRACTIONS

The Art of Staying Focused When All Hell Is Breaking Loose In Your Life

Felix Anderson

DOMINATE YOUR DISTRACTIONS™

Email requests to team@mrfelixanderson.com.

Ordering Information:
Quantity sales. Special discounts are available on quantity purchases by corporations, associations, and others. For details, contact the publisher at the email address above.

Published by GWW Publishing Company

Printed in USA

First Printing, 2018

ISBN: 978-0999197554

DEDICATION

To every setback, hardship, and hindrance in my life, THANK YOU for the experiences you taught me. To the dedicated Wake Your Successful Self Up™ Family and Supporters, THANK YOU for your love and loyalty. To the AMAZING person reading this book, THANK YOU for believing in the words I speak and the words I write. I pray they help you WAKE YOUR SUCCESSFUL SELF UP™ so that you can DOMINATE YOUR DISTRACTONS!!!

TABLE OF CONTENTS

FOREWORD

Blessed is the man that walketh not in the counsel of the ungodly, nor stands in the way of sinners, nor sits in the seat of the scornful but his delight is in the law of the Lord and in his law doeth he meditate day and night. Psalm 1:1-2 KJV. This scripture characterizes Mr. Felix Anderson. He has a very strong prophetic anointing on his life to release captives, awaken the sleeping and stir up great faith in those who hear the voice of the Lord through his mouth. His fearlessness to go against the grain and challenge popular opinion in His messages —to follow the counsel and revelation of God's word — is evident that he takes delight in the law of the Lord and meditates in it day and night

Upon my first observation of him, I knew that he had a powerful word to deliver to those who would receive it. It is this type of willingness and refusal to compromise under the pressure of status quo that causes a man to rise from obscurity —into great prominence.

It is Mr. Felix's character of commitment and courage that draws many to his message of Wake Your Successful Self Up —I am sure that as you read through this book you too will receive an impartation of the same spirit of God that is on his life to WAKE YOUR SUCCESSFUL SELF UP! If you are going to dominate in any area, sphere, industry or field, this implies that you are going to have to be on top and ahead. To dominate means that you have a commanding influence and that people are impressed, inspired out-run by performance. This means that you are the standard and that your work sets the bar. At this level of success you must be confident in your ability, know who you are and always press to do better, go further and dig deeper. Dominate has a root word, that word is "do". This means that in order for you to dominate, you must first do something.

—OSAZEE O. THOMPSON,
AUTHOR, PRECISION PURPOSE
CERTIFIED LIFE COACH,
WWW.OSAZEETHOMPSON.COM

INTRODUCTION

We live in an age of distractions. Remember how "back in the day" you had to pull over and use a phone booth outside the gas station if you wanted to check in or reach out to someone? Maybe this was antiquated by the time you were born. Remember, writing directions down on a piece of paper or pulling out a map in order to get to your destination? This again may have been antiquated for many of you by the time you were born. Oh, and dare we forget when we felt big time with our "pagers." Even the ease of texting has evolved from the day when, if we wanted to type the letter "C", we had to hit the number one key three times, A, B, C. The mentioned examples show us two things which will be outlined in this book. The first being that you cannot remain stagnate and refuse to change if you want to dominate your area of expertise. You must be willing to make the shift mentally to develop ideas and you must be willing to make the shift emotionally to detox from anything causing you not to move forward on those ideas. What I'm about to say is part of my daily declarations over my life when I get stuck on doing things a certain way and when I refuse to let something go. Your inability to detach will impact your ability to develop. You must detach from the distractions if you are to develop mentally, emotionally, financially and more importantly spiritually.

No matter how hard you try, distractions will always be there. It is a matter of how you acknowledge the distraction and immediately go back to what you are doing that matters. If you acknowledge that distractions will surround you at all times, you can plan to minimize them. Those that you can't control, you can focus on ways to better manage them so that they won't be a distraction in the future. As you embrace this journey to DOMINATING, remember these words…FOCUS ON YOUR FOCUS.

~ Felix M. Anderson

WYSSU™ CREED

I AM SUCCESSFUL BEYOND MEASURE!
I BREATHE SUCCESS, LIVE SUCCESS
BECAUSE I WAS BORN TO BE
SUCCESSFUL
I THINK SUCCESSFUL THOUGHTS
I SPEAK SUCCESSFUL WORDS AND I
MAKE SUCCESSFUL DECISIONS
I ONLY CONNECT WITH SUCCESS
MINDED INDIVIDUALS
I REFUSE TO BE AVERAGE BECAUSE I
WASN'T CREATED TO BE AVERAGE.
IF I WANTED TO BE AVERAGE I COULD
HAVE STAYED IN BED
AND BECAUSE I AM AWAKE
I CHOOSE TO EMBRACE AND OPERATE IN
EXCELLENCE.
I CHOOSE TO WAKE MY SUCCESSFUL
SELF UP
SPIRITUALLY, MENTALLY, PHYSICALLY
AND FINANCIALLY.

I SPEAK TO THE CORE OF WHO I AM AND
I SAY TO MYSELF AND THOSE WHO ARE
AROUND ME....
WAKE YOUR SUCCESSFUL SELF UP!

Your next season will require a next level mindset and it may require some new friends.

~

Dominate Your Distractions

CHAPTER 1

ZONE OUT

LET NOTHING DISTRACT YOU AND GET YOU OFF COURSE. YOUR DESTINY DEMANDS THAT YOU DOMINATE DISTRACTIONS.

Dominating your distractions is more than just drowning out the outside noise. It is possessing the ability to become so in sync with the core of who you are and what you're purposed to do that nothing or anyone can get you off centered and off your game. It's about becoming so transparent with who you really are that when people come in the sphere of your influence, they will be able to see your purpose and they will know when you arrive, you have come to facilitate that purpose without hindrance. They will know when you step foot in the building, you have come to do one thing and one thing only- DOMINATE!!! When you master the art of dominating your distractions, everything that is around you will simply be a blur, because the vision you are purposed to birth out of you won't allow you to see anything else. Your thoughts will be clear, which will enable your decisions to be clearer.

Distractions must be mastered, minimalized and if possible eliminated if you are to achieve success in any area of life.

It requires a delicate ear to know when the frequency of a sound is coming to alter the scales of success or cause you to make a detour to your destiny. The sounds that are not in pitch must be muted immediately because they are in violation of your purpose. If the vocal vibrations of the words that you hear coming either from your mouth or the mouth of others do not generate life and make what's in you come to life, they must be muted.

Just like your heartbeat, your words have a rhythm. This rhythm causes everything within you and around you to flow in and out of your life so you can produce that which is essential for your development. During your journey to dominating your distractions, you will become accustomed to saying NO frequently, as it will be the generator of your peace and the foundation to mastering this art. You will encounter engagements, assignments, entrances as well as exits.

It is important to commit to memory the next sentence that is about to be shared for the sake of your peace and your focus. Turning down some engagements is just as important as accepting some assignments.

Know which doors to enter and which doors to exit. DOMINATE YOUR DISTRACTIONS is indeed an art and the principles outlined in this book will give you everything you need to paint the perfect picture of focus in your life.

"Sometimes the things that are most painful can be most helpful because they teach us what not to do and who to stay away from."

~

Dominate Your Distractions

CHAPTER 2

TO HELL AND BACK

THIS IS ONLY A TEST....

Sometimes life just happens. It happens to teach us about others and ourselves. It also leaves scars, which serve as blueprints for us to know how to navigate through hardships. Sometimes when life happens, we experience a glimpse of heaven on earth and many times, we go through pure hell. You have to remind yourself that this is only a test. You need to uproot to upgrade and you must never be afraid to walk away. You may have to separate so that you can elevate. This is where you must have the courage and strength to tell those that are connected to you, who may mean well but are not good for you, "YOU'RE NICE but you AIN'T NEEDED." Let silence be your greatest clap back and you must be willing to be misunderstood by those you love and those that love you. Truthfully, you will have to fire some friends.

What's important is maintaining balance and not allowing personal relationships to become so distractive that they prevent you from progressing and propelling at an optimum level. Sometimes the hell in your life can come by default, bad decisions or disguised distractions. Disguised distractions are the things that look good in our lives but are designed to destroy us. They lure us in with the perception that they are beneficial when in all actuality they are detrimental.

They have one goal and that's to strip you of everything that you are purposed to produce for the good by trying to rob you of your identity.

They are designed to take you to hell and back, leaving you feeling defeated and depleted. Under no circumstances must you allow this to get the best of you. Under no circumstances should you replay the hell in your head because it will only hold you hostage to your disguised distraction. Under no circumstances can you allow anything to get you off your game. You are always in control even when you are going through pure hell. Take some time to get away and get recentered so that you can dominate your distractions.

What was meant to destroy you has no power over you. The very thing that tried to take you through hell is more afraid of you than you may be of it. The fact that you are reading this and that you are breathing is proof enough of what tried to destroy you, could not and cannot conquer you. God Almighty has you covered.

The devil will disguise himself as an angel of light to keep you in darkness. Don't be fooled by how pretty it looks or how good it sounds. As you embrace this journey, I pray that God will show you the hearts of people. The ones that have hidden motives, secret agendas and especially the ones that mean you no good. I pray that your dreams are not destroyed because of TOXIC seeds sown by people who are familiar with you or "think" they know you. Everything that the enemy stole from you and even the people he used to steal from you will have to pay back. Even those that leech off you and don't invest in you will have to pay you back. Even when people try to take you through hell, you have the responsibility of loving the hell out of them from a distance.

Don't be deceived. Your next level of success will come with next level hell and next level distractions. Be prepared for them both.

No matter who does you wrong, it is your responsibility of maturity to always do the right thing.

~

Dominate Your Distractions

CHAPTER 3
MASTER ME

YOU CANNOT DOMINATE YOUR OUTWARD PURPOSE UNTIL YOU DOMINATE YOUR INWARD PERSON.

So often we go through life wanting to master things so we can have this great sense of accomplishment. We begin the repetitive cycle of doing things we enjoy over and over again. It becomes part of our daily psyche-how we identify ourselves and what we are known for by others. Even Jesus asked the question, "Who do men say that I am." This question was not asked from him not knowing who he was, but it was birthed from a place of openness to be able to hear how others viewed him. So are we to be as we seek to become masters of who we are purposed to be. We must be open to hear and receive the opinions of others whether we agree with them or not. We must be open to consider the opinions of others whether they line up with how we identify ourselves or whether or not their thoughts identify with our purpose. Those that are closest to us are reflections of what we are doing right in our lives and can reveal areas where we need to improve.

Knowing how others view you is crucial to mastering yourself. It gives you permission to look into the areas of your life through the eyes of others that you may have overlooked or simply chose to ignore. It puts you in a state of nakedness that says, “I didn't know I was perceived that way. I didn't know I sounded like that when I responded to others with my timing and with my tone. I didn't know I came off as being offensive when I had no intentions of doing so." In life, we must surround ourselves with those that mirror our spirit, our hearts, our goals and our visions. We must surround ourselves with those that are willing to tell us the truth at the expense of falling out with us. We must surround ourselves with those that are not afraid to answer our candid questions truthfully without us being succumbed to the temptation of getting offended and defensive. Like Jesus, we must ask those close to us, "Who do men say that I am?" We must then listen intently not to respond with words, but respond with actions by changing for the better. The questions that you must ask yourself are, "Am I disciplined enough not to be distracted and am I disciplined enough to make the necessary changes to become better?"

"Discipline"; from the Latin 'disciplina' meaning "teaching, learning," and "disciples' meaning "pupil." The 'Art of Discipline' is an action of respect, which means to look at what one is doing to one's self. "Respect' is from the Latin 'respectus,' literally, "the act of looking back." This is why we see the etymology of "discipline" tied in with "disciples' meaning "pupil."

Discipline creates "In-tuition" (intuition), or the "inner price paid" since "tuition" is the price paid for instruction. Your next level of living whether you choose that to be good or bad will come with a price. Choosing to dominate your distractions and your current environment will come at the price of you saying "NO" to many things and many people. This price will demand that you sacrifice and go the extra mile to clean up everything that is disorderly in your life.

Whether it's an unclean home, unclean office, unclean thoughts, unhealthy eating lifestyle, unorganized financial records, unhealthy spending or unhealthy relationships, you must commit to saying NO regularly and frequently.

You cannot effectively say NO to not having peace within and NO to not having peace in your immediate space without becoming disciplined. Keep in mind that people will always respond to you the way in which you respond to yourself so you must always treat yourself well. Saying NO provides you the opportunity to generate self-love so that others can love you as you love you.

Remember that your inability to say NO comes with a price and this may mean that you will lose some things and some people in your life. Don't lose sleep over what you lost and who left. You can lose time, you can lose money, you can lose friendships, but you CANNOT AFFORD to lose YOU!!! If God allowed you to lose it then rest in the fact that He's going to replace it with something better so don't stress yourself out over lost stuff.

The beauty of being disciplined is that when done properly and consistently, it produces results that sometimes take time.

Being disciplined creates an environment of simplicity and simplicity breeds prosperity. Simplicity breeds freedom just as having too many things generates bondage. Simplicity brings joy and balance in your life whereas having too many things whether in our mind or environment can generate frustration, anxiety and fear. Remember that simplicity is an inward reality that results in an outward lifestyle. Both the inward and the outward aspects of simplicity are essential. We deceive ourselves if we believe we can possess the inward reality without it having a profound effect on how we live. To attempt to arrange and live an outward lifestyle of simplicity without the inward reality leads to chaos. Your distraction is your enemy. Until you are able to paint the picture in your mind that greater is available for you, your distraction will continue to dominate you instead of you dominating it.

Strong people are just people who have learned how to navigate through life's issues with a smile.

~

Dominate Your Distractions

CHAPTER 4

MINDSET RESET

YOU MUST INGRAIN IN YOUR MIND THAT ABSOLUTELY NOTHING WILL STOP YOU FROM BEING THE BEST VERSION OF YOU THAT YOU CAN BE IN LIFE.

Your mind is the gateway between what you see in the unseen arena that hasn't become reality but what you wish to become reality. Everything is trying to get your mind's attention. The pull comes from the past and the future, but the goal is to stay in the now. I believe the most powerful thing on the planet is the human mind, so why not learn how to use this powerful tool to the best of it's ability?!

WHAT IS A MINDSET?

World famous sports psychologist Michael Gervais defines our mindset as a particular attitude or disposition to something that's about to happen, and a purposeful mindset has intent, control and will that you're implying about how you want to experience the future moment. So a mindset literally is a filter and a projector. As a filter, your mindset filters how you interpret what's happening in your life. As the projector, your mindset projects the way you want to be in the future.

The stagnation you may be feeling in your life is a direct result of unfiltered thoughts and poor projection. In order to dominate your distractions, you must be able to project and filter properly.

If you think about approaching anything in your life, whether it's public speaking, conquering a fear, taking a test or dominating your sport, you need to ask yourself this next question.

WHAT IS THE MINDSET I WANT TO HAVE?!

There are many mindsets out there. We can have a resilient mindset, an abundant mindset, an aggressive mindset or the millionaire mindset. World famous Psychologist Carol Dweck has taught us that most people have either a Growth Mindset or a Fixed Mindset.

If you have a fixed mindset, you believe that you are great or you are flawed. If you have a GROWTH mindset, you believe that your greatness or your flaws are a result of your actions, and you believe that other people's greatness and flaws are a result of their choices and actions.

WE CHOOSE OUR PATHS AND WE CREATE OUR MINDSETS!

It doesn't matter what happens in our lives. What matters is how we choose to filter these events and create the mindset of learning, growing and developing from every situation. You must have it ingrained in your mind that absolutely nothing will stop you from being the best version of you that you can be in life.

Scotty Reardon lost his leg in a farming accident at the age of 12 and his life changed forever but he learned to set his mind to courage, determination and resilience and became a multiple World Champion in 2 different sports. Can you imagine the physical pain and mental trauma that took place initially?

As with any traumatic event in your life, you must do like Scotty did and get over the hurdle of the hurt and reset your mindset to dominate. You cannot allow what life did to stop you from doing what needs to be done. It's easy to get discouraged but the discouragement cannot and should not override your determination to be great!!!

WHATEVER YOU HOLD IN YOUR MIND CREATES YOUR FUTURE!!!

Start to think about how you want to BE in your life, not just what you want to do. We are human beings, not human doings. Your mindset dictates how you experience anything. You have the control and the ability to learn how to set your mind in preparation for your real life external environment. Your mindset is your internal environment and it's your gift that you take with you everywhere you go and want to be, so why not take the best prepared version with you?!

HOW DO WE SET OUR MINDS?

You need to be clear on what your ideal mindset is for the events you're stepping into in the future. If you need to be calm and collected for your speech or presentation, practice being calm and collected in a controlled environment…

Bbbbrrrreeeaaattthhhheeeeee!!!

If you need to be competitive in an event or workplace, practice your competitive mindset in an environment that you can control so when you step into the external environment or so called reality, you have the tools to set your mind for that situation. This is why I have those around me affirm themselves by saying "Good God I'm Great."

I firmly believe that you should believe you're the best at what you do and if you don't then what you are doing is a waste of time.

DO YOU WANT TO SURVIVE OR DO YOU WANT TO THRIVE?!

When people say you create your own destiny, what do they actually mean? When you create the mindset for every situation in life, you are creating your destiny. This requires a certain level of focus and pressing that is outside the norm. This requires you learning how to ignore people and things well. You can see their mouth moving but you don't hear a word they are saying. You can see the obstacle in the way but in your mind, you have predetermined all of the ways you will go around it. Become so locked into what you are doing that you become the very thing that you are doing and nothing and no one can get you off course. Will this be easy? NO! Will it be worth it? YES!!!

ONCE YOUR MINDSET CHANGES EVERYTHING CHANGES!

Your dedication to staying disciplined in the darkest moments is what really matters. Surround yourself with people that won't let you make excuses.

~

Dominate Your Distractions

CHAPTER 5

DOMINATE YOUR HABITS

"HABITS CHANGE INTO CHARACTER"

~ OVID

Most of us don't realize how much power our habits have. Not just because accomplishing anything requires continuity and discipline, but also because habits are an investment of energy and time. I remember the day when the realization that "time + energy = your life" hit me like a ton of bricks! I've become much more selective about how to spend both ever since. Think about how much time and energy you invest in what you do on a regular basis and what that says about your life.

Whether it's the work you do for your job or business, the people or pets you take care of, a yoga or exercise routine or the things you do for fun. They're all reflections of where you're at in life. Now let me ask you, is it where you want to be? If you're a new parent, your habits are going to be completely different than if you are a single person starting a new career, or if you got married and lost your job, or if you just retired and are searching for a new purpose.

The thing about life is that our habits seem to sneak into our life almost unwillingly. So we either rely on them to provide stability, we take them for granted, or we struggle with them because they turn into meaningless routines.

No matter what type, habits accumulate time and energy. They're like a bank account you invest your life in. I'm not just talking about action-oriented habits; your mental habits go into the account as well because they're also energy. How much time and energy you spend criticizing, complaining, judging or procrastinating also speaks about where you are mentally and emotionally. Again, is it where you want to be?

When you consciously create new habits, as an investment in yourself, your goals, and your self-growth, then it's another story altogether. You get to harness its power to shape a life with purpose. You can utilize the energy and momentum they accumulate to accomplish your dreams and aspirations. You can feel the energetic path they build under your feet because they get you closer to where you want to be.

So I invite you to make a list of your mental, emotional and physical habits, and reflect on what they say about where you're investing your energy and time. You can put them on a vision board or write them in a journal just to release and get them out of your system if you feel like having fun with it. Be honest with yourself and recognize what you give the most power to. Is it yourself or others? Is it your dream or someone else's? You must also ask yourself how many of your (mental or emotional) habits distract you from accomplishing your goals? Try to find ways to "recycle" the energy of the habits that pull you away from your goals and start creating new ones that keep you on track. Don't be like those people who suddenly go out jogging after years of living sedentary lives and give themselves a heart attack!

Be gentle and compassionate with yourself, but be firm and committed at the same time. Take small steps, energize short routines, reorganize small chunks of your day. More importantly, no matter what you choose to do or for how long, don't stop. If you are consistent, the energy you invest will build up to carry you through your own resistance (yep, there's always resistance when we have goals) and get you where you want to be. It's another way of giving your inner voice a stronger presence and a greater impact in your life. The definition of a distraction is anything that comes between you and your goals. If it doesn't take you closer, then it's dragging you away. As the saying goes: "If you want to defeat someone, distract them." Yet, when you're working alone, you can easily think that a couple of minutes to make a quick call or open some mail won't make a difference. Then one thing leads to another, and if you're like me, you end up far from where you wanted to be after an hour has flown by.

Sometimes life fast-forwards like a movie screen run amok. I'm in one of those phases right now and it's forcing me to become better organized and more sensitive to the ways I allow myself to be distracted. I've learned that giving in to distractions is a choice. As I become conscious of the little things that I allow to take me away from a given task, I see more clearly that every "allowance" is a choice. Truth be told, the only way to manage potential distractions is to control two things: Your environment and your own actions. You can choose to eliminate distractions by finding or creating a work environment that helps you to focus and that shields you from distractions, whether visual, sound or even smell. Choose what works best for you. Do you prefer some background noise and a bit of greenery out your window, or are you happiest working in a quiet setting? Perhaps you do best in a coffee shop, or prefer to do certain tasks in a bookstore. Peronally, I do some of my best writing and thinking sitting at the park for clarity and in the coffee shop for creativity.

Creating an environment that keeps you focused is half the battle; the other half is choosing to master your work habits. Do you multi-task and jump from one task to the next? If that's the case, set a timer to help you stay focused on one task until it's completed. Then reward yourself and set it again. You'll be amazed at how much you can accomplish in seven minutes. Six minutes and 60 seconds is what I give myself for each daily task. Seven (6 minutes and 60 seconds) sessions of focused, productive work within each hour will change your life. Stay with the routine of setting a timer until it becomes a habit. Like a muscle, focused attention is something you can develop with time and practice.

Distractions can't always be avoided. Those who focus win the game; whether it's on the golf course, the basketball courts or in your home or business office. In each case, keeping your focus long enough to finish a task well is a choice. Everyone who seeks to be successful has to choose whether they will be master of their actions and thoughts, or let outside influences control their habits.

Your choice to allow distractions to interfere with your goals is nothing more than a habit that can be changed by choosing to create new habits. Eben Pagan said that "Habit is destiny." Master your habits by building new focus muscles that will keep distractions away, and then watch your productivity go to the next level. Think of the time you spend thinking about a particular problem in your life.

Your mind wanders and pretty soon you are thinking about something else entirely. You start thinking about a conversation you had and what you should have said. You may start thinking about what other assignments you need to do. Just like that, you've lost 15 minutes or even more. Add up all the time you wasted on these random thoughts and you'll soon see that a quarter or even half of your time is utterly wasted on distractions.

Think how much more productive you could be if you could concentrate fully on getting the current task done. You would have more time to do other things that you prefer doing. Your "to do" lists would be shrinking instead of expanding. The key to dominating tasks is to focus on your focus!

Developing this one habit that would allow you to quickly place distracting thoughts in the background could make a huge difference in your life. So, start developing that habit today. According to Dr. Rob Gilbert - First we form habits, then they form us. Conquer your bad habits, or they'll eventually conquer you. Do you have habits that may prevent you from achieving success? If so, it is never too late to change your habits because in order to conquer your bad habits, you must replace them with good habits and become disciplined. This is easier said than done so I want to share with you what has worked for me in my quest to remain disciplined. I will share with you the following HABITS I have developed to assist in achieving success.

The Health Habit

Being in good health will provide you with the necessary energy you need. You only have one body. One major purpose of the body is to carry your brain. Take care of your body and your body will take care of you. You only have one of them.

The Attitude Habit

Have a positive attitude in all that you do. Regardless of the circumstances, remain steadfast in being positive. If you don't think you can do it then you will not. Your attitude will carry you further than you realize when you remain positive. Believe in your dream because if you do not, no one else will.

This habit comes from your positive attitude. You must believe that whatever goal you have set for yourself, you will achieve. You will make your dreams come true. You must believe not only in your dream but also yourself.

Self-esteem and self-confidence all come from believing that you are supposed to be happy. You are worthy of all the success you desire. You must believe this!!!

The Intent Habit

When you set a goal, your intentions have to be clear. Developing the habit of intent causes you to focus your efforts on the task at hand. This becomes key when developing your plan to achieve your goal. You will never account for all obstacles that you may face on your journey. Your intent will keep your goal at the forefront of your mind thus you will remain focused.

The Tenacity Habit

When you encounter failure, tenacity is what keeps you going. You must not fear failure. Failure is a part of the process to achieving success. What you learn from failing is how to succeed. Tenacity is how you overcome your fear of failing. You will not quit. Nothing will stand in your way. Nothing will defeat you.

Sure Habit

Being sure of yourself, your dream and your goal means you are sure to succeed. It is the last habit because it encompasses all the attributes of the previous habits. You are sure to succeed when you take care of your health. You are sure to succeed when you have the right attitude. You are sure to succeed when you believe. You are sure to succeed when your intentions are clear. You are sure to succeed when you are tenacious in pursing your dream.

Make sure your character and your conversation know each other.

~

Dominate Your Distractions

CHAPTER 6

DOMINATE YOUR TIME

If People Do Not Respect Your Time then They Don't Respect You.

This is what enables us to engage in effective self-management. The will is key to "time management", but keep things like determination and discipline in mind as well as we go down the following principles. They are crucial to managing your time effectively. It's not time management, it's self management. Time management is often the buzz word, but that's really not what it is, because you can't manage time, you can only manage what you do with the time given to you. But you must remember this important distinction if you are to succeed. You don't manage time, you manage yourself. Again, this is elemental to my mantra of everything begins within you. Time simply is a sense of discipline that originates within you. The successful person doesn't enjoy doing particular things any more than the unsuccessful one but their disliking of certain tasks is overshadowed by their sense of purpose and achievement. My dislike of people wasting my time is what causes me to better manage my own. Because I manage my own time well, I refuse to allow those that are negligent with their time to be negligent with mine.

Immediate Response

This area of self-management can be boiled down to a handful of ways. There are tasks or action steps that need immediate response and there are a lot of them that don't. A good example would be the phone ringing. It's not often one can bypass the automatic response to answering it. Now people are reluctant to even sit at a meal without setting the cell phone on the table so as not to miss any type of message. I have this mantra concerning the phone and feeling the need to want to and have to answer it all the time...if it's important, they will leave a message. You must determine in your mind to set clear boundaries as to when you will and when you won't answer calls without feeling guilty about it. Again, if people don't respect your time then they don't respect you. When it comes to calls, people and your time, there clearly are levels. Know where to place your priorities, for the key to life is balance.

Level of Importance

Other activities outside of those that subjectively may need an immediate response are more important matters. These are the tasks that you actively prioritize within the frame of a project or goal to be accomplished. Remember, you must have clarity in your to-do list, as well as your prioritization of that list. Keep these two concepts in mind when you are developing a schedule or a work flow. When it comes to self-management, one of the most effective ways of organization is to break things down into sections. Those would be: Important, Not Important, Necessary and Not Necessary Right Now. Be careful not to be run down or beaten by the Important List. Many people are dominated by this section.

If you keep your focus on everything being important all day long, very shortly you're going to burn out. Many people try to escape by doing other trivial or menial tasks but you must develop a balance. If you think positively and operate like successful people do, you will be more opportunity-minded, not problem-minded. Work proactively, plan ahead and use preventative maintenance.

Turning a Day into a Week

I've often said that when work and tasks start to pile up on you, plot things out on a weekly basis. Remember, you're organizing yourself away from "crisis", and proactively getting into prevention. You can still prioritize on a daily basis, but enable yourself to spread action steps out through the week. This allows you to cultivate more of that balance I alluded to earlier. It enables you to widen your focus out of crisis mode and still get to the other important things as well.

Remember to Delegate

This is a harder thing to do for a lot of people. Find people who excel in certain things that you do not. Delegate tasks in areas where other people have those specific skills and interests. By doing this you're allowing yourself to do what drives you and what your overall passion is. In turn, you're also allowing others to engage their skills and take active roles in their interests.

Cultivate a team effort. No truly successful person "arrived" totally on their own. They all have a collaborative team that works in conjunction to achieve their goals. You are the captain and you're the one to see that everything is working in sync.

You are the one with the overall plan, guidance and vision. You must learn to work smart. Utilize others talents so that you can work to avoid a crisis and operate with more balance.

Whatever you decide to pursue, remember that you won't become self-sufficient over night. New businesses need time to take root, generate a client base, and become profitable. Patience, as we all know, is a virtue. You can use time to your advantage to brush up on your skills or get your business recognized. Trust me, it will all be worth it when you receive your first payment. The sense of satisfaction knowing that you, on your own time and of your own free will, are able to provide something that can serve people well is well worth it!

WISDOM TO STOP PROCRASTINATING AND MAKE TIME FOR SUCCESS

1. Decide to make time for success. Don't cop out by claiming you're too busy. The reason many don't have success is because they don't make time for it.

It's a fact that most people devote more time to spending money than planning their future.

You probably waste more time worrying about the circumstances in your life than actually taking positive action to change your life.

As the saying goes, "If you want something done, give the task to a busy person."

~ BENJAMIN FRANKLIN

It may be that you need to work on your time management skills and do a better job of budgeting your day. Before you go to bed every night, make a list of things that need to be accomplished the following day. We all have things that need to be done every day, but make one of those small tasks yours to help you build your future. You should never be too busy for You!

2. Track Your Day. If you really don't feel that you have an hour a day to become successful, try this exercise: for three days, keep a time log. As you go through each day, write down the things that you do and the time you spend on them. Make sure you write everything down. Track everything to the minute. Believe me, by the end of the second day, you'll start to be embarrassed by how much time you waste.

You may be surprised how much time you spend every day on social media. Aimlessly surfing the web for no real purposes can be extremely unproductive. Having a well-developed social media strategy is one thing, but simply wasting time is not. Everything you do must be done with purpose and on purpose.

3. Turn It Off. Turn off the TV, unplug the phone, stay away from the video games and turn off your computer. Your family might protest at first - but if you get them involved, by the end of the month your kids will be finding different ways to be successful. Get your family talking about goals and discovering ways to achieve them. You can act as each other's accountability partner. If you don't feel comfortable making this a family activity, find like-minded friends and meet with them once a week for a "mastermind" meeting.

Once you do this, you'll be surprised how quickly you progress towards your desired goals.

4. Don't let anxiety win. When it comes to getting success, many people procrastinate simply because the whole process makes them nervous. Don't let that happen to you. No matter where you are in life at this moment, that is only a single moment in your life. Thousands of people who are worse off than you have used these techniques and triumphed over adversity. Believe in yourself, take a deep breath, and follow these strategies one at a time.

5. Remember that there will never be a better time than NOW. Things won't be better tomorrow or next month if you keep going along the same way as you've been. Do you know what my definition of insanity is? Continuing to do the same things you know don't work and hoping for a different result. Don't make the same mistake of thinking things will improve on their own. They won't. So don't wait.

Stop trying to explain your agenda to people who are not on it. Focus on who and what matters.

~

Dominate Your Distractions

CHAPTER 7

DOMINATE YOUR SUCCESS

"As important as it is to follow the success patterns of those that have went before you; it is even more important to make sure that you BLAZE YOUR OWN TRAIL!" ~ Rudeco Roberts

Our potential in life is not determined by uncontrollable circumstances and settings, racial or gender characteristics, or even economic conditions or access to knowledge. Never give in to the mentality or believe the dominating culture which ingrained into our minds that our potential is determined and success is the result of the schools we graduated from, jobs held, awards won, degrees earned, wealth acquired, or any credential or certificate obtained. Success and potential are created, developed, and determined within ourselves. They result from the foundational laws of success: determined desire, ability to dream big, belief in self and in the dream, complete commitment to the goal, overcoming the voices of fear and failure, daily action and persistence, learning from and getting up after failures, and never quitting until the goal or dream becomes a reality.

Unfortunately, far too often we allow our culture and society, educational system and workforce, literature and media, as well as peers and even our own family members convince us that success is measured and potential is determined by certain qualifications. These fallacious qualifications range from GPA's, to standardized test scores, institutions attended to education obtained, work experience, to titles held, social connections to family heritage, and from the color of our skin to the anatomy of our body. Undoubtedly the GPA's and degrees obtained, etc. are important and will help on the journey to success, but they alone are irrelevant and will prove insignificant if the laws of success described above are not understood, believed, and implemented as well.

Do you really believe that you can literally, become and accomplish anything in life? Your successes, greatness, and potential are determined by you alone; and all of the characteristics necessary to achieve your goals and dreams already lie within you. If you realized how capable, brilliant, talented, beautiful, and powerful you really are (or could be), it would not only astonish you, it would inspire you.

I have found that most people are not ignorant of this reality, they just willfully choose to ignore it because they are afraid of their own potential or they are not willing to put in the work necessary to achieve it. Ben Herbster summed it up perfectly when he penned: "The greatest waste in the world is the difference between what we are and what we could become."

Never forget, however, that in the journey to reach our potential, dreams, and successes in life, it is desire, belief, action, and persistence that are essential.

You alone must discover, create, and determine your own potential. Gone must be the days when we mistakenly follow the masses and believe the misconceptions of what actually determines our potential and success in life. Your full potential is reached, successes are achieved, and your dreams and goals are realized if you can understand, believe, and implement the laws of success - think big, believe more, act now, and never quit!

- Have you ever wondered why some people can sell just anything, but you can't?

- Have you ever wondered why some people are so successful, and you aren't?

- Have you ever wondered how some people can just make money, but not you?

- What's the answer? What is the secret? Why them and not me?

The reason is because they have learned the power of the mind and the power of personal persuasion. They have control of their emotions and they know when to pause and they know when to pursue. They see opportunities better than most, and they can see failure as a means of success. Yes, they have control of their mind, and understand the "Power" of Personal Mind Dominance.

So, you ask, how did they get this control? This persuasion, this mind power? Let me help you understand the power of sharing. They learned it from special information handed down from father to son, they studied the contents of this information that can teach you how to train the brain to be successful in business, through the "power of thought" and they made themselves rich. The power of the mind is immensely strong and by training the brain or mind, to dominate your thoughts you and anyone can then start to think in a different way. Approach things from a different angle and begin to see things in a different way.

You will begin to see opportunities that you never saw before than can change your outlook on life. You start to think like a business man, and as soon as you do, changes to your life can start to happen for you too. For years, successful and rich business men who had been fortunate enough to study such information and learn the secrets, knew the power of such information that made them successful. They wanted all the riches and success for themselves, so they decided to hide this information away from the eyes of the general public.

These powerful mind changing secrets were reserved for a selective few of privileged eyes only. They didn't want the man in the street to get too knowledgeable and undermine the power they held over people, business, and commerce. But not any more because all of that has changed and the lids of knowledge have been blown off and the secrets have now been revealed. You hear a lot about the power of positive thinking and other motivational systems. In truth, it really is a matter of knowing where you want to go in order to reach your goal. But have you ever considered the hidden attempts from others to get control over you and your mind? Why do they want this control you ask? The answer is simple. Your mind is the most influential weapon known to man. Your mind simply cannot be controlled or contained by anything or someone outside of you - no matter how impressive it or they appear to be.

Tyrants throughout time have tried to restrain others, but the capacity of the imagination is just too influential. I'd like you to take this into account as you consider those around you: someone who tries to talk you back down to their rank of accomplishment - is a tyrant. As Victor Hugo said, *"An invasion of armies can be resisted, but not an idea whose time has come."*

So if your time has come, what's the true problem here? It is YOU! Your own choices where you have permitted others to "suggest" their limitations onto you. This is occasionally referred to as Crowd Consciousness. To break out of this, you must first take responsibility for everything in your life. When you do this, you will learn that the capability to respond will come forward from within you. NEVER, EVER - blame anything that has "happened" to you, on anyone else but yourself! Anytime you blame someone else, you are giving them comprehensive control over your mind.

Once that happens, they have taken command over the success of your home, your business and your life! To persist with assured change towards accomplishment, become aware of any "victims" close to you and steer free of them. When you watch television, or listen to music ask yourself: Is this a situation of lack, or success? If it is not success, it is lack or disappointment and exposing yourself to it will eventually influence you to think in that direction.

A victim is a lure for situations of "lack". They will bit by bit, insidiously, but indeed most assuredly - convert you into a victim too. When that happens, success stops flowing into your life, and everything that you have worked for will drain away bit by bit. Take notice of those who cheer you and those who don't. Steer free of those who don't encourage you in your home business and NEVER EVER tell them about anything that you want to accomplish. Here's a helpful way to think of this: The root word of confidence is "confide". This is a sign for choosing who you ought to surround yourself with. Every single thing that you do, think or say each day contributes to your success rate.

If you are determined to build a stable and abundant life, read the following wisdom for success. Keep in mind that they will only go as far as your mind-set will allow them. So it is important that you remain positive, determined, and focused as you work towards your goals.

WISDOM FOR SUCCESS

First, accept that 'success' and 'ambition' are not bad words. It is only human to want prosperity and stability. We have a right to maximize our potential and earn as much money as we possibly can. So don't let your distractors put you down.

Make peace with yourself. Learn to forgive yourself for any mistakes you made in the past. Tell yourself that you deserve a second chance, and that you will do better.

Know your passions and interests. Can you picture yourself working in a job you dislike just for the money? That goes against even the tips for success shared by successful career people and entrepreneurs.Those people did well in their respective fields because they loved and enjoyed what they were doing. If you are doing something that you love, a strong work ethic comes naturally to you.

Be an enthusiastic learner. Learning did not stop when you left school. Learn on the job. Learn from your own mistakes and the mistakes of others. Get rid of your fear of failure by trying new things. Read up on the things that interest you, whether they are of a personal or professional nature.

Nurture relationships with people who matter. Your success relies on the strength and quality of your relationships. Surround yourself only with positive family members, friends and colleagues. Choose mentors who generously share tips for success rather than selfishly keep them a secret. Do not trample on people to get to the top. What goes around comes around.

Get rid of the following negative words and thoughts: "I can't"… "I'm afraid"… "I don't think that's possible"… "I'll try" … Get these words out of your vocabulary. You have the ability to do what you are determined to do once you eliminate the fear factor.

Do not procrastinate. Each day we have a checklist of the things we need to accomplish. Do them. No ifs or buts. Finishing tasks on time builds character and discipline, which will come in handy when you start taking on bigger responsibilities in both your work and personal life.

Be patient and thankful. Greatness is not achieved overnight. Continue the good things you are doing and be grateful for each little success you earn each day.

Pay it forward. As you find yourself slowly but steadily reaching the top, share your tips for success to others. You contribute to a better world when you help more people.

Never confide something to a person who does not boost your confidence. To do so will result in your own confidence vanishing away and you will grow to be another constituent of the victim crowd. Once that happens, you are doomed to lack the success you require.

My desire is that this helps you to take back control of your mind. Stop giving dominance of your mind over to others! Do this, and you will most assuredly see changes in your life, and find the success that you deserve. The only thing now to make this happen is for you to make it happen. Whenever you give others the power to control your thoughts, you give them the power to control your life. Learn how to think for yourself and make your own decisions. You should always seek counsel and the wisdom of others, but you are the one that ultimately has to make the decision that you will have to live with.

What others view as failure is just a successful person's detailed instructions on what not to do next time.

~

Dominate Your Distractions

CHAPTER 8

F.O.C.U.S.E.D.

DISTRACTIONS ARE SIMPLY AN INDICATION THAT YOU ARE ON THE PATH TO GREATNESS!!!

Focus requires both forgetting and remembering. While this may appear to be difficult, it is actually a process that makes focusing easy. Forgetting past pain isn't the easiest thing to overcome, especially, if the wound is fresh and those that have done you wrong are seen daily. Forgetting isn't easy when you've invested your all and you have been kicked out of an environment suddenly. Forgetting isn't easy when you have invested love that has yielded no return on your investment. If you are to dominate, forgetting isn't an option, it is a mandate. This is never easy, but once you get over this hurdle, you will be able to heal. As strong as you are, you must give yourself permission to feel then forget. During the process of forgetting, you do not need any "I remember when we and you use to" people around reminding you of things you are trying to forget. Especially, when you have clearly moved on to something better. Again, focusing requires both forgetting and remembering. Forget the “Who's” that did it, what happened and remember “Why” it happened.

Opposition: In order to strengthen your focus, you will need opposition. Whatever you are pregnant with must require an element of pain before it is birthed. Your focus is no different. In an ideal world, we would want nothing and no one to bother us when we are working on desired goals. In an ideal world, you would have peace and quiet whenever you need it and however long you need it. That is the ideal world but not the one in which you and I live. Instead of viewing the outside noises and distractions as enemies to your focus, embrace them as tools purposed to help strengthen your focus. They will help you apply the principle of forgetting to remember constantly.

Applying the principle of forgetting to remember will help you to keep working without pausing and constantly starting and stopping over and over again, as this will cause you to waste time. Often times our distractions come unnecessarily through invitations we have inadvertently presented prematurely to those with perverted agendas. These invitations come when we fail to shut down conversations that have extended too long. They come when we fail to shut off those who have clearly revealed their true intentions yet we brush it off because we want to give them the benefit of the doubt. Understand that you cannot give anyone the benefit of the doubt because there is no benefit in doubt. In order to DOMINATE, you must know when to SHUT IT DOWN and SHUT IT OFF.

This includes family, friends, conversations and habits that cause you to lose focus. This can be offensive to some who are not connected to you or those who are not in sync with your day-to-day activities. It is important to verbally and properly articulate your plans to those in your inner circle where you are mentally and emotionally during your SHUT OFF and SHUT DOWN phase. It helps you to maintain peace and avoid unnecessary opposition.

Many have become accustomed to shutting off the outside noise that causes us to become distracted. What I've found to be the most difficult thing to do is to shut off the inside noise that causes us to doubt our ability to succeed. That little voice inside of you telling you what you can't do, how you're not good enough, how you won't make it IS NOT from God. Silence it NOW!!!

Concentrate. In the world with constant distractions, precise concentration must be mixed with purposeful calmness. Precise concentration sends a message to the inner you that says, you are in control of this matter regardless to what is around you. It's the constant mind rehearsal that serves as the gentle reminder of why you are doing what you are doing in the first place. Your purposeful calmness gives those around you the confidence they need to believe not just in you but in themselves as well.

Calmness is contagious as it is what I like to call the *Energy of Confidence*. And this confidence whether you have it or not will be revealed during times of conflict. This confidence is the true mark and common denominator between those that are successful and those that remain mediocre. Your ability to remain concentrated and calm during chaos will cause you to conquer whatever is purposed for you to defeat. When your focus is fixed, favor will have a way of finding you.

Understanding your why cancels unnecessary commentary. The commentary in your head that tries to talk you out of pursuing your dreams. The commentary in your head that's constantly telling you that you're not good enough. Commentary from unaccomplished critics shouldn't concern you. When you understand your "WHY", the who, what, when, and where will eventually find their way to help you facilitate your purpose. Concentrate on what you're purposed to conquer because focusing on foolishness will only slow you down. You are here on earth for a purpose and the key to understanding your purpose is knowing your why.

Who you need to be there will be there when you need them to be there. What you need when you need it will be there when you need it. How it will get done will get done when you take your first step. Concentrate on mastering each moment of the process and the very thing you are wishing to see will manifest through your consistency.

Strength only counts when all hell is breaking loose. It is in your dark moments, it is in your dark times where you will find out what you are truly made of. It is in the valley where you obtain discipline. It is in the valley where you build stamina, it is in the valley where you learn about character, it is in your valley where you learn who is for you and who is against you. Listen to your experiences as well as the experiences and the mistakes that others make. There are some lessons you don't have to learn because you may not have the strength to recover from them. During your process of learning how to focus, you will learn and find out that you are stronger than you think you are.

You will learn when to speak up and when to keep quiet. Never underestimate your own strength. A crisis will reveal the strength of your character or the level of your crazy. Don't be ashamed to hit the "RESET" button in your life. Sometimes we start poorly and need to begin again simply because we allow our emotions to get the best of us.

Get your FOCUS back so that you can FINISH STRONG!!!

Emotions and Energy are the driving forces to staying focused and both must be managed well. Dominating your emotions are perhaps one of the most important thing's that you'll need to dominate. These emotions can be the gateway and the difference between you breathing life and you breathing death on your situation. You cannot dominate if you are not in control of your emotions. You cannot dominate if you are easily swayed. You cannot dominate if you are overly concerned about the words of those whose thoughts, words and actions are antithetical to your purpose.

Should you care what others say? This is a Yes and a No answer. You should care when their words prompt, provoke and promote you to do better and be better. You should care when their words exploit areas in your life that need improvement that maybe you can't see. On the flip side of this, you shouldn't care at all because their words good or bad will not determine your mobility to make a difference in your life. If their voice is louder than your voice when it comes to you making changes, then their voice will be the cause of your collapse if you are ever faced with pressure. Never let the words of critics good or bad get so ingrained in your head that it causes you to become distracted.

You cannot always determine what will pull on you but you can determine whether you'll be in or out of your feelings. Becoming overly concerned about what people think can blur your vision causing you to get in your feelings. Don't let your feelings make you forfeit your favor and cause you not to believe in you.

There is a difference between being in control and having control. Life is guaranteed to happen, and when it does while you may not have control of the situation you must pre-determine in your mind to always remain in control of your emotions. What happens on the exterior should not always impact what goes on in the interior but somehow it does, causing many to become discouraged.

Discouragement is something that sneaks into our lives without warning. It can hide behind clothes, makeup and hair dos. It's so bold that it will even hide behind a smile. You pretend like everything is all right when it's everything but all right. Discouragement will always ride to work with you. Discouragement doesn't care who you are. Its only concern is to try to derail you off the course to your destiny. If you listen to discouragement, it will cause you to make bad decisions. Particularly painful is discouragement in the life of the believer.

As we travel from season to season, it is not just the perils we face but it is seeing the wicked go forward while the righteous are held back. Sometimes we see people succeeding that don't PRAY as hard or work nearly has long have not been faithful at all and it seems like they have moments of victory placed in close proximity so that we can see it.

Their victories seemly flaunted in your face not while you're having a similar experience but while all hell is breaking loose in your life. While you are going through agony and tragedy, others seem to be having victory. Sometimes it's not your test that baffles you, but how they are succeeding and you're not that makes you lose focus.

You cannot let what life throws at you stop you from giving birth to what's on the inside you. You cannot let discouragement and conflict shake your confidence.

Purge any thoughts of discouragement immediately. When you're in the process of dominating your distractions you will sometimes miss it. Some days will be better than others and all will go well and sometimes you will just flat out get it wrong. Don't be too hard on yourself as none of us are perfect and while none of us are perfect, this does not exclude us from operating in excellence.

The key to purging is to learn what is beneficial in your life. You learn how to do this through everyday living. If it feels overwhelming at first, start applying the principles within the first week of the month. Add a week as you see progress in reaching your goals. The key to purging is distinguishing between what you are attached to you and what you are assigned to during this phase of your life. A key element to purging is setting the proper boundaries. Set Boundaries Quick!!! Don't allow other to make you feel guilty for setting the necessary boundaries you need to stay focused. Everyone is not assigned to you in this season. Protect your emotional energy by not entertaining that which is not in alignment with where your vision is taking you. Knowing when too much is too much is important when dominating your distractions.

Everyone has limits and it is important to know yours and make the adjustment before your emotions take you to a place that jeopardizes your future. Knowing your triggers and your environment will prevent you from being unnecessarily distracted. Doing the mental preparation before you engage in situations you know will be anxiety provoking is important.

This will cause your automatic reactions to be less abrasive and destructive. When you are consumed with where you are headed in life, you won't allow anything in your past or present to prevent you from being positive. Will it be easy, absolutely not and this is why I am challenging you to PRESS to be POSITIVE!!!

Sometimes you have to forget who you were in order to remember who you are purposed to become.

The sacrifice you are making right now may not be easy but it will be well worth it.

~

Dominate Your Distractions

CHAPTER 9

DOMINATE YOUR THOUGHTS

WHEN YOU GET A REVELATION OF WHO YOU REALLY ARE, YOU WILL NO LONGER THINK SMALL.

Proactive thoughts are important to acquiring your success and your success cannot exist without them. Consider Webster's definition of success: 'a desired or favorable outcome'. All outcomes are determined by actions. Actions require decisions to act and decisions are merely decisive thoughts. Therefore, it is easy to conclude that the thoughts that dominate your mind will dictate the actions you take, and the results you generate. Your mind never stops forming tomorrow's reality. As estimated, a human being has over 60,000 different thoughts a day. Many of those thoughts are contemplations, hopes, wants, and fears of tomorrow. No matter the type, every future based thought is another piece of the reality that you accept to be inevitable. Your destinations cannot change until your thoughts change.

Don't make the mistake of underestimating the importance of what you are thinking today; it will be your reality of tomorrow. Constantly bombard your mind with thoughts of what you want, and project them into the future. This should feel good to you, so don't overwhelm yourself by attempting to control your every thought. If you are thinking of things you want in the future, you are right on track.

If you want a better future, you have to more effectively direct your thoughts today. Successful people, expend most of their thoughts focusing on the future-proactive thoughts.

One of my favorite quotes is from Napoleon Bonaparte when he said "take time to deliberate; but when the time for action arrives, stop thinking and go in." Ralph Waldo Emerson was quoted: "Thought is the blossom, language the bud; action the fruit behind it." It is hard to find a historical icon that did not strongly advise others to assume proper thought when aspiring to higher achievements. There are drastic differences between the way highly successful people and extremely unsuccessful people think and their outcomes.

Imagine if an extremely unsuccessful person began to avoid the earn-to-spend mentality, clearly defined their desired success, pursued their goals rapaciously, and refused to fail-or if-a successful millionaire no longer defined his success, relied on excuses for failures, failed to take required actions, pursued only easy/quick successes, and gave up when things became too hard. Both of their lives would immediately begin to move in completely different directions.

Success, and failure, is simply the outcome of habits that are motivated, and acted upon by contrasting paradigms of thought. Successful and unsuccessful people first think, then act, and then attain completely different results in their lives and their finances.

Proactive thoughts create your destination. A proactive thought is a contemplative thought of the potential future. No matter how impossible or distant your goal might seem in the beginning, it will seem increasingly more attainable as you think about it more. Your mind is a magnificent tool that leads you to the materialization of what you proactively think about most. If your thoughts are inundated with fear of what might occur, your mind will assume that is the outcome that you desire.
If you think about something often enough, you will

eventually fail to see any other possible solutions. You will ultimately find yourself forcibly drawn towards the impending outcome that your mind considers most often.

It is safe to surmise; changing how you think today will determine who you are, and the success you attain tomorrow. There are four levels of thought that I refer to as **THE SEE SAW PRINCIPLE:**

1) What You Want To See: these are positively charged—proactive thoughts. They are thoughts of what you want in the future.

2) What You Can't See: these are negatively charged—proactive thoughts. They are thoughts of what you do not want, or want to avoid in the future.

3) What You Saw: these are positively charged—reactive thoughts. They are thoughts of what you liked, or enjoyed in the past.

4) What You Hate About What You Saw: these are negatively charged—reactive thoughts. They are thoughts of what you did not like in the past.

Each level has productive uses, however, thoughts that fall into "What You Want to See" should dominate your mind most of the time. "What You Saw" and "What You Hate About What You Saw" are essential to learning and growth. "What You Saw" and "What You Hate About What You Saw" contain the thoughts in which you learn what you should not do again, how to become more effective, and how to rewrite goals. Negatively charged thoughts will attract negative emotions, and expectations. This is why you must choose to stay focused on that which is positive. Remember that what you see with your eyes is where your mental focus will be calibrated which will impact your emotions and determine where your physical journey will lead. Reactive thoughts dwell on the past, and are very unlikely to breed thoughts that can help you in the future.

Proactively positive thoughts bring positive emotions, confidence, energy, and creative ideas for accomplishing your goals.

It is said that Thomas Edison failed to invent the incandescent light bulb over 10,000 times. When asked how he persevered through so much failure, he replied "I have never failed; I simply found 10,000 ways not to invent the light bulb." Obviously, they all learned from their past challenges, but they chose to live on the "What You Want to See" level.

Constantly increase the amount of time you spend in a proactive and positive state of mind. Let these thoughts consume your mind and failure will be a thing of the past. Historic icons of the past believed strongly in the importance of proper thinking in acquiring success, and perseverance. What others view as a 'failure' is just a successful person's detailed instruction on what not to do next time. Stop dwelling on the past, and the things you don't want. Learn from your mistakes, and then move on.

I am telling you to think positively and to think in future-tense as much as you can.

"A man is but the product of his thoughts, what he thinks, he becomes."

~Mahatma Gandhi

Your personality is a combination of your beliefs and your values. The way in which you think and act are behaviours that you have developed in response to key events or circumstances that happened during your upbringing.

Your personality has been influenced by the things you have learned about life from other people, mainly your family. Your personal experiences in the past and the stage of life that you are at are also part of these influences.

THINK POSITIVE, ACT POSITIVE

AND

YOU WILL LIVE IN ABUNDANCE.

Your past will always make a cameo appearance when you are on the brink of your breakthrough. STAY FOCUSED!!!

~

Dominate Your Distractions

CHAPTER 10

DOMINATE YOUR PAIN

WHEN YOU GET A REVELATION OF WHO YOU REALLY ARE, YOU WILL NO LONGER THINK SMALL.

Healing starts where acknowledgement begins. In order for you to experience proper healing there much be a formal announcement that you need to be healed. The time for reliving and rehashing what use to be and what could have been only prevents you from living out and fulfilling what can be. When we choose to continue to relive our past experiences that have cut us deep, we are choosing to subconsciously pull the scab off of a wound, making it fresh all over again.

You owe it to yourself to stop picking at the things that have caused you pain and give it time to heal properly by leaving it alone. Don't permit people and things in your life to serve as a reminder of your past failures!

You've gone in circles long enough, your destination is right around the corner, and it is waiting on you to arrive. What hurt you before can no longer hurt you again. It's time for you to get up and make some changes because the next chapter of your life can't be written until you close the chapter that you're in right now.

Dominate every distraction that comes your way by making up your mind to focus on who you were purposed to be and do what you are purposed to do.

As you embrace this new journey of staying and remaining focused, I want you to begin by forgiving yourself for allowing past pain to make you get out of alignment with your purpose. You must make the daily decision to elevate above every distraction as you

WAKE YOUR SUCCESSFUL SELF UP!

FORGIVE YOURSELF

For sharing your heart with people who couldn't hold its contents. forgive yourself for making excuses for people you should have been excusing out of your life. it's not always a person's fault for letting you down. sometimes it's because our expectations of people can be unrealistic so when the unrealistic expectations go unmet, we become frustrated and eventually hurt. when they let you down once, don't open the door for them to disappoint you again. As you embrace the road to your healing, be careful of trying to rekindle relationships that God has specifically told you to release.

QUIET TIME

~ Wisdom List ~

1. Start your day early before the spouse, kids and emails make their demands for your time and attention.

2. Sit still and quietly as you begin to engage and navigate to a place of peace. There you can hear for your instructions and DIVINE DOWNLOADS.

3. Write down your instructions and meditate on them. Give them priority and focus. Always approach your alone time with pen and paper because the instructions you receive in your alone time may only come once. These instructions while they may be simple, can produce major changes in your life.

4. In this time it is not important to be in the past or the future but it is important to be in the now so that you can be in the know.

N.O.W. K.N.OW. T.H.I.S.

~ Wisdom List ~

N – Never pay more attention to the things around you than you pay to God above you. Everything in your environment is subject to change when you change your spiritual and mental outlook on it.

O – Do not overthink about where you are purposed to be and who you are purposed to have in your life.

W- Work with what you have and do not overthink the process to the point where you do not do any work at all.

K- Knowing what to do is half the battle. Your now moment provides you with the knowledge to proceed.

N- It shows you what you need and who you need. Those that need to be there for you when you need them will be there for you when you need them.

O- In the NOW, you get the opportunity to receive divine downloads necessary for your next level.

W- Your now moment gives birth to wisdom whether in your alone time or dealing with something in real time. drowning out the outside noise will give you the wisdom to handle every situation.

T- Take more thought into consideration and know that sometimes things in your life just have to happen in order for you to purge properly.

H- Had it not happened, you might still be in the cycle of constant distraction causing you not to have clarity of thought.

I- It, them, her, or him had to leave because they were destiny blockers.

S- Seasons change and seasons are an indication that you are beginning something fresh that will bring about change. NOW is the TIME for you to KNOW that THIS is your season to change and for you to….. DOMINATE YOUR DISTRACTIONS

Let nothing and let no one cause you to become so distracted that you cannot fulfill what you were put on this earth to do. Give no man and give no woman that much power over your life.

~

Dominate Your Distractions

ABOUT THE AUTHOR

Felix Anderson is an Author, Brand Advocate, Speaker, Success Architect and Founder/CEO of The Executive Concierges. He is the author of the best seller, Wake Your Successful Self Up and The Wake Up Call: 13 Days to Waking Your Successful Self Up. After his mother was murdered at the hands of domestic violence, he became a voice for the voiceless and was selected as a Man of Character for his role in helping fight domestic violence. He is a health enthusiast and leader that possesses an undeniable energy and practical wisdom; distinctiveness like no other with the mission to teach you how to better serve yourself and those around you. Felix and his wife, Tina, live in Mississippi with their two sons.

Made in the USA
Monee, IL
26 October 2023

45230813R00059